Princess Anne
Champion of Europe

PHOTOGRAPHED BY SRDJA DJUKANOVIC

TEXT BY BERNARD FOYSTER

FOREWORD BY ALISON OLIVER
TRAINER TO H.R.H. PRINCESS ANNE

London · Arlington Books
in association with *The Daily Telegraph*

PRINCESS ANNE
CHAMPION OF EUROPE
First published 1972 by
Arlington Books (Publishers) Ltd
38 Bury Street, St. James's
London S.W.1.
in association with
The Daily Telegraph

© Srdja Djukanovic
and Bernard Foyster
Made and printed in England by The Garden City Press Limited
Letchworth, Hertfordshire SG6 1JS
ISBN 0-85140-209-7

FOREWORD

I am delighted to have been asked to introduce this book. For me, personally, it recalls many of the happy, tense and exciting moments of my association with Princess Anne in her riding career. In his splendid photographs, Mr Djukanovic has captured many incidents at events where Princess Anne was riding which spectators and television viewers will have missed. He portrays the tenseness and comradeship of the riders, as well as illustrating something of the strain of competition at this top level. In the accompanying text, Mr Foyster recalls in detail the steps by which Princess Anne has advanced from her early days in Pony Club competitions to the stage where she now competes on equal terms with the best riders in the world. I am sure that this book will provide a permanent souvenir for all those people interested in riding in general and in the success of Princess Anne in particular.

Alison Oliver.

Author's Note

My grateful thanks are due to Alan Smith, Equestrian Correspondent of The Daily Telegraph. *I have relied heavily on his informative and colourful reports and I am grateful to him for his kindness in reading the proofs of the Three-Day Event sections of this book.*

Bernard Foyster

1

The show-jumping ring at Burghley on the final day of the European Three-Day Event Championships. Into the ring rides a slim, fair girl just twenty-one years old. A vast crowd—some estimates put it at 20,000—surround the arena. There is complete silence as the young rider begins the most vital round of her short career. Gently she urges her horse forward. They clear the first fence, then the second. The atmosphere is charged with tension as one by one the obstacles are safely negotiated. One more to go—and the whole arena erupts as they sail over the last fence. No faults, a clear round—and Princess Anne Elizabeth Alice Louise, in the lead from the first day and never headed, is the new European Three-Day Event Champion. There to see her triumph and to present the champion's trophy to her are her mother and father, the Queen and Prince Philip.

Success by Royalty at the top-level of international sport is comparatively rare. King Constantine of Greece has sailed for his country in the Olympic Games; Princess Anne's own grandfather, King George VI, played lawn tennis at Wimbledon; her cousin, Prince Michael of Kent, has represented his country at international level in the dangerous sport of bob-sledding; and, of course, her father, Prince Philip, is an international-class polo player. But power, position and privilege mean little in the sporting arena. The best coaching, the best equipment, even—in

7

the case of riding events—the best animals are not, by themselves, guarantees of success. It is the determination, the very character of the competitors that matter. And these are things that cannot be bought.

In her career, Princess Anne has actually had to overcome disadvantages that never affect the ordinary competitor. Not for her the opportunity of learning her exacting trade in obscurity. From the first, even as a child in Pony Club events, when it became known that she was competing, in would flock the crowds. All eyes would be on the Royal competitor. Other young riders could make their mistakes without exciting comment—but not Princess Anne. If her pony or horse refused, or if she were unseated, it called for front page headlines—even though the incident was unremarkable in every way, except that it had occurred to the Queen's daughter.

A typical report might read:

> Princess Anne fell from her horse at the X, Y or Z horse trials yesterday. She was unhurt and remounted. Later she walked to her car and drove off. Her fall came as her gelding, Purple Star, refused a five-bar gate. After remounting, the Princess took Purple Star over the gate and three further fences. But she collected 11 jumping faults, which put her out of the championship.

Just consider the basic news value of the above if it had happened to anyone other than Princess Anne. Occasionally, too, there have been incidents which have been reported widely, not so much for what actually happened but perhaps for what was reported to have been said at the time. Just such an incident occurred in May, 1970 at the three-day Army horse trials at Tidworth, Hants, where Princess Anne was unhurt after a fall.

Reports published at the time went on:

> A Buckingham Palace spokesman was asked if he had any knowledge about a report that the Princess said: "I saw bloody stars." He said: "No, I'm afraid I haven't."

Now whether Princess Anne actually made that remark or not is immaterial. It is a perfectly innocuous sort of thing that might well have been said by anybody involved in such an incident. And, again, if said by anyone other than the Queen's daughter, it certainly would not have excited comment. In fact, for the record and on the best authority, the word was *not* said. . . .

This, then, is the glare of publicity under which Princess Anne has been forced to follow her favourite sport. For any rider, competition in public brings nerves to a peak of tension. For a young, untried rider to have to operate under these additional difficulties must have been nearly intolerable. But Princess Anne had to learn her competitive riding under just such conditions—and, as a result, has obviously benefited, emerging as a tough competitor, filled with a steely determination to give of her best, come what may.

Someone who gets really upset when people say that Princess Anne has had every advantage on her side is her trainer and friend, Alison Oliver, wife of Alan Oliver, the show-jumping champion.

On training, Mrs Oliver points out that the average daily stint for most members of the British team is about three hours. Not so for Princess Anne, who is expected to travel the world carrying out her official duties. Princess Anne has to visit Mrs Oliver's training stables near Windsor in Berkshire, when she can fit in the time. And with engagements to carry out all over the British Isles, to say nothing of Royal tours abroad, this is not always easy to do.

But quite apart from all this, Princess Anne's triumph at Burghley last September was the more remarkable for the fact that she was not completely fit at the time. In the pre-Olympic year, when every event took on added importance, when a carefully worked-out programme was building steadily to a climax, disaster struck. In July, just two months before the European Championships, came the shock announcement from Buckingham Palace that Princess Anne had been taken to hospital for an emergency operation. In the King Edward VII Hospital for Officers in Marylebone, she underwent an operation for the removal of an inflamed ovarian cyst from which a haemorrhage had occurred. The operation was performed by a team led by Sir John Peel, the Queen's gynaecologist. Sir Ronald Bodley Scott, the Queen's physician, was consultant.

The first hint of the Princess's illness had come earlier in the year during a Royal visit to Canada in May with the Queen, Prince Philip and the Prince of Wales when the Princess had been unable to carry out some engagements in Vancouver at the peak of the tour. At the time her illness was officially dismissed as "the sort of trouble that affects many travellers". But there was renewed concern when it was learned that she had undergone medical treatment by doctors aboard the Royal Yacht Britannia.

There was no further hint of trouble until the dramatic announcement of her admission to hospital only a day after she had mingled with guests at a Buckingham Palace garden party.

On July 7, the day after the garden party, she complained of feeling unwell and Sir Ronald and Sir John were called to the Palace to see her. Later that day she missed a wedding to which she had been invited at the Queen's chapel at the Savoy—and in the evening she was taken by Royal car to hospital. Plans for the Princess to compete in the £500 Rothman's Trophy on July 21 at Wembley's Royal International Horse Show were cancelled. The careful programme leading up to the European Championships at Burghley was shattered. But this major setback served to reveal the iron determination the Princess possesses.

Mrs Oliver recalls visiting Princess Anne in hospital soon after the operation was carried out. She says: "Personally, I had given up hope of her competing at Eridge in August (the final trial for the European Championships) only to find her sitting in a chair making plans for a crash get-fit course in order to be in time to ride."

The Princess left hospital on July 17 and went straight to Windsor to convalesce, all public engagements having been cancelled to the end of the month. Five days later she moved to Balmoral, where her convalescence continued. So, too, did the Princess's self-designed crash keep-fit course. And on August 20—just forty-four days after her major operation—the Princess did indeed ride at Eridge Park.

Nobody could reasonably have expected her to return to competition so soon after a serious operation and to strike her best form. Yet at the end of the first day, which saw the completion of the advanced dressage and jumping events, Princess Anne's name was at the top of the leader board. Not only that, but in the dressage test she had shown considerable determination in overcoming continuous, upsetting rain.

In the show-jumping phase, her horse Doublet had one fence down—number seven, the planks—and also collected two time penalties, but their final score of 42.33 was beyond the reach of their rivals. This was a quite incredible return to top-class competition—and there was so nearly a fairy-tale ending but one mistake in the cross-country cost the Princess dear.

At fence number eighteen, the Princess and Doublet did not jump the water too well and Doublet stopped at the uphill fence away from it. Brought in again, perhaps too tightly, he straddled it and Princess Anne slipped from the saddle. The 20 penalties for a refusal and 60 for a fall pushed them back to twelfth place. But for that they would have stayed in front. But really it did not matter. Princess Anne had signalled her return to competitive equestrianism in no uncertain manner. Despite the setback of the operation and the interruption to her training schedule, she was ready to compete against the best riders of nine nations at Burghley.

2

Princess Anne was born into the age of modern communications, when words are transmitted round the world in a flash, yet the announcement of the birth of a second child to Princess Elizabeth, as the Queen then was, and Prince Philip, had a cosily old-fashioned air about it. The news that a second child had been born on August 15, 1950 to the Royal couple was conveyed by means of a simple notice hung on the wrought iron gates leading from Clarence House into The Mall. Members of the public waiting outside pressed forward eagerly to read: "Her Royal Highness the Princess Elizabeth, Duchess of Edinburgh, was safely delivered of a Princess at 11.50 am today. Her Royal Highness and her daughter are both doing well."

Princess Anne was the first Royal baby to be born at Clarence House since it was converted from an old portion of St. James's Palace in 1825–27. She was born in a room on the second floor, overlooking The Mall and St. James's Park. Her cradle was the same one used for her mother, Princess Margaret and Prince Charles. The baby made her first public appearance on September 17, 1950, when she travelled by train to Scotland from King's Cross, her mother holding her up for the crowds to see.

The name Anne was a reversion to a Royal fashion of Stuart times. The Princess was also given the names Elizabeth, Alice, Louise. Elizabeth was shared by her mother and grandmother, Alice was after Princess Andrew of Greece, her paternal grandmother, and was also one of the names of the Princess Royal, and Louise was the name of the eldest daughter of King Edward VII, the Duchess of Fife.

Princess Anne's first birthday was spent on the Balmoral Estate—later to be the scene of many happy, relaxed holidays. Before she was two, the Automobile Association made her their one-millionth member. The reason? The AA reckoned they reached this milestone in their membership at about 12.30 pm on August 15—about the time the Princess was born.

In addition to this early membership of the AA, the baby Princess had two waltzes composed for her and a street and chrysanthemum were named after her. The waltzes were written by Kenneth Pakeman, a former BBC programme engineer and assistant music director in the Midland Region. It was Biggleswade Urban Council in Bedfordshire who decided in October, 1950, to name a road on a housing estate Anne Street to commemorate the Princess's birth. The chrysanthemum was winner of the trophy for the best specimen plant at the National Chrysanthemum Society's show of greenhouse-grown chrysanthemums which opened at the New Horticultural Hall, Westminster, on November 4, 1955. The prize-winning plant, entered by Mr H. T. Burtenshaw, of Worthing, had eighty blooms of soft pink and salmon colouring.

The day before Princess Anne's second birthday, British Railways announced that a passenger express engine was being named after her. The locomotive, Number 46202, had been converted to the "Princess" class for use on the main line route from Euston to the North. The fishermen of England were not to be outdone either, a trawler named Princess Anne being launched at Beverley, Yorks, in August, 1952.

The next year saw the Queen's Coronation and, still only two years old, the blue-eyed, blonde Princess appeared with her parents on the balcony of Buckingham Palace. Earlier, the inquisitive eye of the television camera had caught some delightful shots of the Princess and her brother staring through rain-misted windows of the Palace at the glittering scene at which their mother was the central figure.

The young Princess's travels continued in April, 1954 when, with her brother, she sailed in the Royal yacht Britannia from Portsmouth to Malta and then on to meet the Queen and Prince Philip in Tobruk. In June of the next year, Princess Anne and Prince Charles flew for the first time when they travelled back to London from Scotland in a Viking of the Queen's Flight. Both of them went on to the flight deck for a time to see the controls. Three months later they saw their first Highland Games when they went from Balmoral Castle to the Braemar Gathering. Princess Anne wore a red pullover and the kilt.

A visit to England in 1956 by B and K—Marshal Bulganin and Mr Khruschev—was marked by the presentation to Princess Anne of a three-month-old bear cub called Nikki. The Princess was reported to have played with the cub for half-an-hour before it was handed on to London Zoo. Incidentally, in July, 1962, a rather sad account appeared in some newspapers to the effect that Pickles, the Zoo's male Syrian bear, had been deserted by his mate Winnie, who had left him for the much younger Nikki. In January, 1963, the fickle Winnie gave birth to twin cubs. Nikki was the father.

Early lessons for the Princess and her brother were given at Buckingham Palace by Miss Peebles, their Governess. In February, 1958, it was solemnly reported that Princess Anne had lost her two front teeth. Cdr Richard Colville, the Queen's Press Secretary, answering an anxious enquiry from an inquisitive reporter, confirmed that this was indeed the case. Rising to the occasion, he added comfortingly: "It is perfectly normal in a child of her age. They will grow again." The Princess was then seven.

General public interest in the Princess's day by day life continued unabated. Even such an ordinary family occasion as a visit to Whipsnade did not pass without comment. The public were informed, through the Press, that the day had gone swimmingly, "with only a pair of lion cubs, who snarl at everyone, refusing to behave with proper courtesy".

Princess Anne did not escape the ordinary childish ailments. In May, 1958, she entered the Hospital for Sick Children in Great Ormonde Street for the removal of her tonsils and adenoids; in April, 1959, she caught chicken-pox at Windsor; and in March, 1961, she had measles.

The Princess continued to be educated by Miss Peebles and on her ninth birthday an end-of-term "report" appeared in the Press. It read:

She continues to do lessons every morning during term time at Buckingham Palace with her governess, Miss Peebles, and her two friends, Caroline Hamilton and Susan Babington-Smith. Lessons cover the usual subjects for a child of her age. The Princess particularly enjoys history lessons and last term started studying the reign of Elizabeth the First. She also enjoys Geography and studying maps. During the Canadian tour by the Queen and Prince Philip, she followed her parents' progress on a map of Canada, flagging the map as they reached each new place. She now has regular French lessons. The Princess continues to have weekly sessions of piano lessons and dancing classes are held at the Palace for a small class to learn ballroom and ballet dancing.

The Princess also has a weekly gym lesson and this term had a few tennis lessons on the Buckingham Palace tennis courts. She is a keen swimmer and bathes as often as possible in the Palace swimming-bath. She was taught to swim by Prince Philip but has not yet learned to dive.

The Princess has a pony at Balmoral so that she can join in the riding there. At Windsor during the past year she has been riding regularly at week-ends, sometimes taking small jumps. She is also a keen cyclist and her bicycle is at Balmoral too.

One of the "great excitements" of the past year for the Princess was the revival of the Buckingham Palace Brownie Pack. After a few meetings, she was duly enrolled as a "Pixie" by her great-aunt, the Princess Royal (President of the Girl Guide Association).

Princess Anne, like most children, enjoys watching television, reading adventure stories and having someone read to her.

The Princess continued to take an interest in the Brownies and, later, the Guides. In December, 1960, she took the part of the first speaking angel in a nativity play given by the Buckingham Palace Brownie Pack in the Throne Room at the Palace. By then, the Princess was a Sixer, or leader, of a group of six Brownies.

Five months later she had passed her Brownie's first and second class badges.

Her leader, Miss Mary Millican, said: "A fortnight ago Princess Anne had to cook sausages and bacon to pass her Brownie first-class test. They were very nice, too. She likes to mess about in the kitchen." Also for the first-class test she laid a fire, cleaned a pair of shoes, tied up a parcel and addressed it for the post, made a cup of tea, showed that she knew the semaphore alphabet and the points of the compass, and produced for inspection a pair of hand-knitted bootees.

Later, in May, 1961, Princess Anne duly became a Girl Guide, twelve Guides of the re-formed Buckingham Palace Guide Company going to the Palace for the "flying-up" ceremony. She spent the next Whitsun weekend under canvas on her first Girl Guide camp "somewhere in Sussex". The site of the camp was kept secret so that Princess Anne and her fellow Guides could go there again without attracting sightseers. Eventually, Princess Anne became a Patrol Leader, wearing Horsewomen's and Swimmer's badges on her right shoulder.

Weddings, especially Royal weddings, are always favourite occasions with the British public and it was inevitable, therefore, that sooner or later Princess Anne would be chosen to act as a bridesmaid. The chance came in January, 1960, at the wedding in Romsey Abbey of Lady Pamela Mountbatten and Mr David Hicks. Princess Anne, who was still only nine, was said to have made "an intent, purposeful bridesmaid". Four months later the Princess was one of eight bridesmaids aged from six to twelve at the wedding of Princess Margaret and Mr Anthony Armstrong-Jones in Westminster Abbey, and in June, 1961, she was bridesmaid at the Duke of Kent's wedding. On April 25, 1963, Princess Anne shouldered the duties of Chief Bridesmaid at the wedding of Princess Alexandra and Mr Angus Ogilvy.

On this occasion she wore her hair up in public for the first time. The Queen's hairdresser, Mr Emile, who had dressed the Princess's hair since she was a small girl, said rather sadly afterwards: "Well, they grow up, don't they?" In September,

1964, the Princess travelled to Athens to act as one of six bridesmaids at the wedding of King Constantine and Princess Anne-Marie of Denmark.

Meanwhile, the Princess's education remained in the capable hands of Miss Peebles, with occasional reports of progress being made public. In July, 1962, she paid an educational visit to France, to the tiny village of Chapelle-sur-Oudon. As the guest of the Marquis and Marquise de Saint Genys, who both spoke good English, the Princess was told: "No English for the next week". The Marquis was a champagne exporter and in the grounds of his Chateau was a race-course where there was horse-racing twice a year, in spring and autumn. On the second day of her stay at the Chateau the Princess went riding on a chestnut horse in the grounds.

In February, 1963, the Princess started to learn Latin, a special tutor visiting Buckingham Palace every week. Then, in July of the same year, came the announcement that the Queen had chosen Benenden, a girls' public school in Kent, for Princess Anne to continue her education. This was a complete break with tradition, the Queen herself having been educated entirely at home. Princess Anne duly arrived at Benenden as a boarder, joining nineteen other girls in the Lower V. To the teaching staff she was Princess Anne, but to her fellow-pupils she was just Anne.

Her stay at Benenden was reasonably successful from the academic point of view. She gained six GCE 'O' levels and two 'A' levels—not enough, however, to take her to University.

During her final year at school she was made a house monitor, wearing an orange tie with blue flash to show her official status. She was one of eight monitors at Guildford House, which had fifty girls. There were privileges that went with the new responsibilities. For the first time in ten terms at Benenden she could turn out her lights at 10 pm, a full thirty-five minutes later than the juniors, and she could also cook up a supplementary meal on Sunday evening, usually eggs, and keep her bicycle at school. After training on cycle maintenance and safe-riding, she passed her national cycling proficiency test.

3

Although there has never been any doubt about her first love at sport, Princess
Anne has tried her hand at plenty of other activities. She has been a regular visitor to
Wimbledon and at one time it was suggested that she might emulate her grand-
father, King George VI, by playing on the All-England Courts. Skating at
Richmond has been another pastime and in July, 1969 she tried water-skiing for the
first time. She was able to remain upright—something most beginners find
difficult—and her brother quipped: "After all, she knows how to ski on snow."
Then, of course, there has been yachting at Cowes.

Actually, Princess Anne's introduction to yacht racing in August, 1964, must have
been a disappointment to her. There was a blazing sun to delight the holidaymakers
but hardly a breeze to help the yachtsmen and, altogether, it must have been a fairly
frustrating initiation in the Royal yacht *Bloodhound*. At one time the Princess, who
wore a blue sports shirt and slacks, was seen assisting in hoisting the sails but much
of the time she kept well out of the way of the crew, leaning against a cabin
bulkhead.

With their father, Princess Anne and Prince Charles travelled to Liechtenstein for
a winter sports holiday in January, 1965. But, unfortunately, the holiday turned into
a game of dodging the attention of persistent French photographers and the oppor-

tunities for indulging in winter sports were, consequently, severely limited. The following January, however, the Princess had a much more successful time with other pupils from Benenden on a visit to Davos in Switzerland.

Princess Anne was baptised on October 21, 1950, at Buckingham Palace by the Archbishop of York, then Dr Garbett. Sixteen years later she was confirmed in the private chapel at Windsor Castle at a service conducted by the Archbishop of Canterbury, Dr Ramsey, assisted by the Dean of Windsor, the Very Rev Robert Wood. Three godparents were present—Princess Andrew of Greece, Prince Philip's mother, the Princess of Hohenlohe-Langenburg, and the Rev Andrew Elphinstone, a cousin of the Queen.

In December, 1964, the first "pop" music party was held in the Crimson Drawing Room at Windsor Castle when the Prince of Wales and Princess Anne entertained nearly a hundred young guests. It was the first party they had given and their guests arrived to find the battlements floodlit and a large Christmas tree lit up outside the Norman Tower. The Crimson Drawing Room, biggest of the Royal drawing rooms at Windsor, had been specially prepared for dancing. The huge red carpet had been taken up. Prince Charles was Master of Ceremonies and the music, supplied by his own tape recorder, included all the latest "pop" hits.

Princess Anne had at least one fairly nerve-racking experience when she first started to drive. In September, 1967, she took the wheel of a shooting-brake on a shopping visit to Ballater in Scotland. The inevitable holiday crowd gathered and gave her a round of applause when she made a smooth start to the return journey to Balmoral some nine miles away. She was obviously a good learner for she passed her driving test at the first attempt on April 17, 1968, after personal tuition by the Queen and Prince Philip and two sessions at the Metropolitan Police Driving School at Hendon. As part of her final training at Hendon she drove three different models of cars on the skid pan. She took her test at Isleworth, driving a red Rover 2000TC from the Royal Mews.

As Colonel-in-Chief of the 14/20 King's Hussars, Princess Anne drove a 52-ton Chieftain tank at Paderborn in Germany. Afterwards, possibly with thoughts of London traffic in mind, she told her instructor: "I would love one of those for Christmas." On the same visit, clad in an army combat jacket, Princess Anne fired ten rounds from a sub-machine gun and got five shots within three inches of the centre of the target. A suitably impressed instructor commented: "Even the best shot in the regiment could hardly do much better". Just to prove it was no fluke, the Princess then took up another automatic and, firing from the hip, put eleven out of twenty rounds in a "terrorist" target at twenty yards.

The Princess again showed her marksmanship on a later visit to "B" Squadron of the 14/20 King's Hussars, when they were stationed in Hong Kong. Blasting away with high explosive ammunition on the Ha Tseun firing range, only five miles from the border with Communist China, Princess Anne displayed "dead centre" accuracy as she fired the main gun of an armoured car, demolishing six targets with as many shots.

Wearing overalls over a silk dress and replacing a broad brimmed hat with a cap, she climbed into an 11-ton Saladin armoured car. One of the 76 mm shells she fired blew up a target minibus. She then fired five smoke shells from the same gun, laying down what an Army officer described later as an "adequate" smoke screen. After that, Princess Anne transferred to the turret, where she fired a .30-inch Browning machine-gun normally handled by the armoured car commander. She kept her finger on the trigger until the belt of ammunition was exhausted. One of the officers who had watched her said later that the princess had produced "some of the best shooting I have ever seen". The Princess was delighted with her accuracy for after she had hit the first target, she exclaimed: "That's splendid. I certainly seem to have destroyed that one."

The officer said that the Princess had done just as well as any man could have done. He had slowed her down when she was firing the Browning machine-gun because she was too enthusiastic!

While at the range, which was in a rural area fifteen miles from Hong Kong city, the Princess also drove a smaller Ferret scout car for about ten minutes. As she walked from the Saladin to the Ferret, she wiped her greasy hands on the seat of her denim overalls.

Having lived her life in this constant glare of publicity, no doubt the Princess was not too surprised when a minor traffic incident in which she was involved while driving her 125 mph Reliant Scimitar sports car attracted the headlines. What happened was described by the other party in the incident, Mr Patrick Ling.

He said that while he was driving in Brompton Road, Kensington, he braked when the car in front of him did so and then he heard "a hell of a loud bang". When he got out a man, who was a passenger in the other car, said, to Mr Ling's surprise: "Send the bill to Buckingham Palace."

"I was a bit dubious", said Mr Ling. "I had heard that sort of thing before. Then the man said, 'This is a Crown Equerry car'. I asked him who the driver was and he said, 'Princess Anne'."

Mr Ling's car suffered a broken rear lamp, a slight dent in the rear bumper and slight damage to one corner of the body. He estimated the cost of the damage at about £25. A Buckingham Palace spokesman said later that damage to Princess Anne's car was "fairly superficial", affecting only the bonnet and headlights. Repairs cost £35.

Whatever the more gushing gossip columnists on some women's magazines might have us believe, British Royalty, generally speaking, is still decently shrouded in privacy. Few and far between are the opportunities for ordinary people to glimpse the real, human person behind the remote, formal Royal figure. Television, perhaps, has done most to break down this particular barrier and some of the more intimate revelations of Princess Anne's personality came in a BBC film she made for the children's programme, *Blue Peter*, during a visit she paid to Kenya as President of the Save the Children Fund.

Princess Anne and Doublet framed by one of the great trees in Badminton Park.

Always a keen and knowledgeable
spectator at polo, Princess Anne arrives
with her brother, the Prince of Wales, to
watch him play at Smith's Lawn,
Windsor, in 1968.

Applause for another
competitor at Badminton.

Prince Andrew, Lt.-Colonel John Miller,
the Crown Equerry, and Princess Anne
watching Prince Charles preparing to play.

Against a background of horse boxes,
Princess Anne relaxes between
chukkers at Smith's Lawn

Prince Charles, Prince Edward and Prince Philip arriving for polo at Windsor.

Serious spectator. . . . Princess Anne watching her father and brother playing polo at Windsor.

*Family outing to polo at Windsor....
With the Queen are Prince
Andrew, Lady Sarah Armstrong-
Jones, Viscount Linley, Princess
Anne and Queen Elizabeth the
Queen Mother.*

A last word with Princess Anne before Prince Charles and Prince Philip join their team-mates.

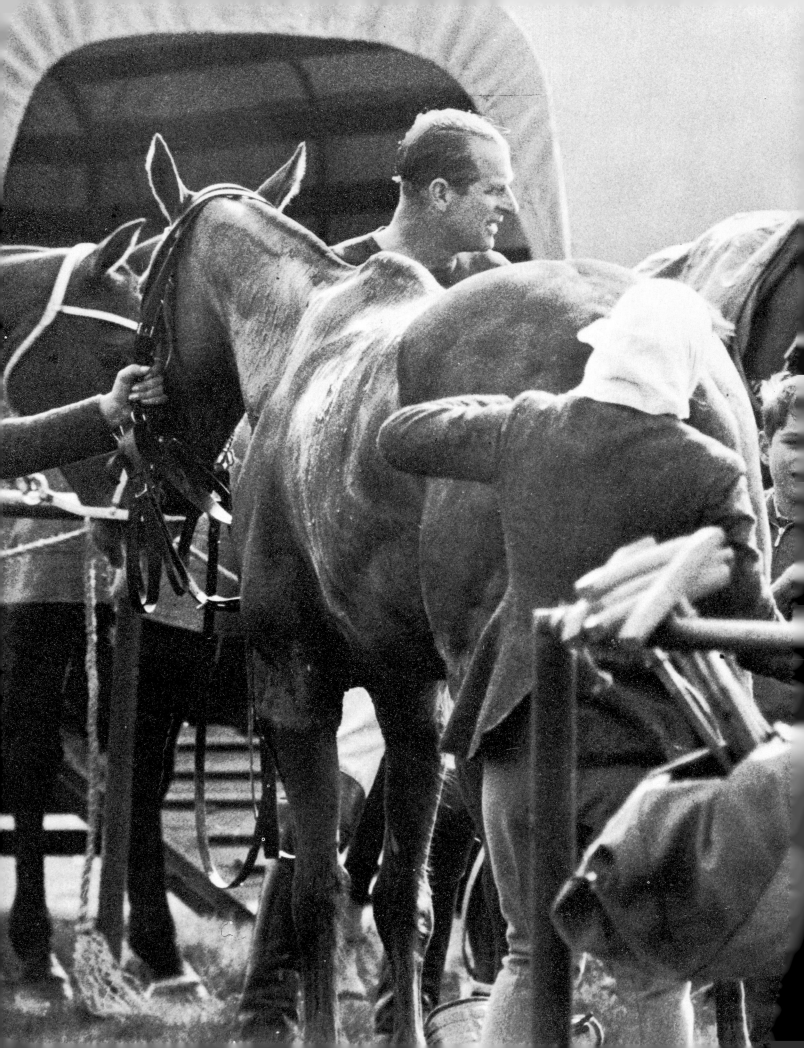

The game is over and Princess Anne and Prince Andrew go "back-stage" to see their father's ponies.

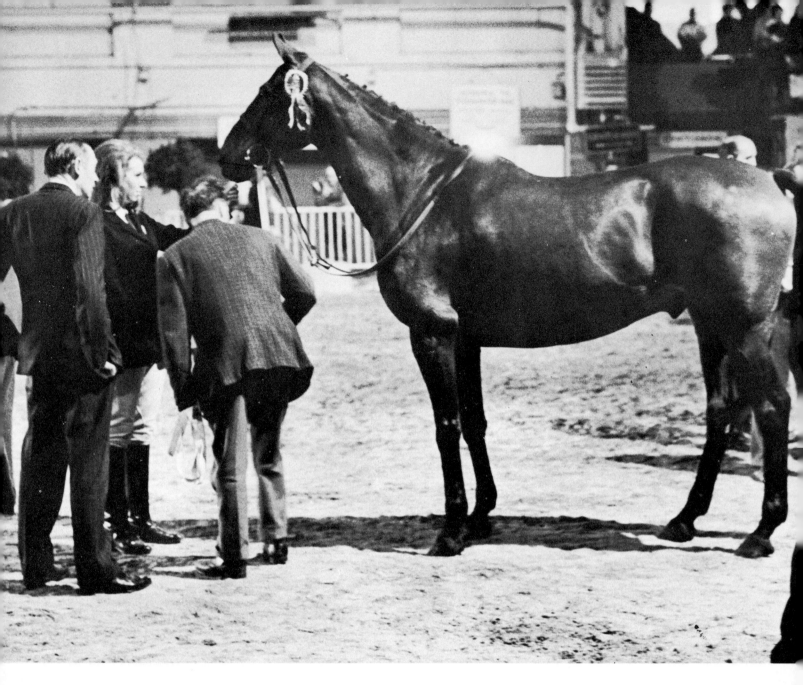

A future champion meets a great champion. . . . Princess Anne greeting the immortal Arkle, greatest steeplechaser of all time, at Wembley's Horse of the Year Show in 1969.

Princess Anne is known to prefer Coca-Cola to wine. . . . She waits by her car at Wembley with an empty can at her feet.

*Princess Anne visiting the stables
behind-the-scenes at Wembley.*

*Walking through the crowds at
Wembley, Princess Anne is followed
at a discreet distance by her
personal detective, Mr. David
Coleman.*

*Princess Anne and her personal
detective, Mr David Coleman,
at Wembley in 1969.*

Visitors to Wembley look at photographs—and fail to notice Princess Anne.

Show-jumping at Crookham.

The casual look visiting stables at Badminton.

The Duchess of Kent with her children, the Earl of St Andrews and Lady Helen Windsor, at Badminton in 1969.

*A neat turn out of both horse and rider
for a dressage test in 1970.*

*An affectionate nuzzle from
Doublet at Badminton in 1970.*

*Princess Anne and Doublet pick
their way through early
morning Gloucestershire mist.*

*Nervous moments while waiting to compete
at Badminton in 1970.*

Princess Anne and Doublet
displaying great style show-jumping
at Badminton in 1970.

Princess Anne's trainer, Mrs
Alison Oliver, straps-up Doublet
at Crookham in 1970.

Show-jumping at Crookham in 1970.

*An anxious glance back after the
show-jumping section at
Crookham.*

*Keeping Doublet limbered up at
Crookham.*

Concentration during the dressage at Crookham.

The dressage test at Crookham, where the judges were looking for "a well-schooled horse, supple, obedient, keen and fit —yet calm."

Princess Anne and Doublet showing their paces in the dressage at Crookham.

Crookham 1971 and only Doublet looks solemn.

The dressage section at Crookham.

Immaculate turn-out of
horse and rider at Badminton.

For example, talking to Valerie Singleton, the programme presenter, who accompanied her on safari, she announced that she was never likely to be seen wearing "hot pants". "There is a limit to what you can do", said the Princess. "And that's the limit. People complain that one is not with it, but honestly. . . . There are certain things I will not do."

She returned to the subject of clothes in her first radio interview—in a recording made for Radio Hong Kong and re-broadcast by the BBC's *The World This Weekend* programme. Acknowledging that her fashion image was "fairly staid", she added that her clothes had "to do the job that I do, which means they have to be presentable and not too way out. I like to choose clothes that are going to serve as many purposes as possible, which means they are not very exciting," she added. This particular recording was made at Buckingham Palace, where she was interviewed by Helene Chung of Radio Hong Kong.

In the forty-minute *Blue Peter* film, the Princess was shown riding, photographing wild life close-up, swimming in the Indian Ocean and touring a centre for destitute boys in Nairobi—and talking frankly and informally.

She recalled her reactions to the Coronation, when she was not quite three. It was, she said, "the normal, sisterly fury at being left behind when my brother went to it—which has been a source of severe argument ever since". She talked, too, of the nine-year gap between her and the younger members of the Royal family.

"I think you can't help being big sister with that sort of gap in age," she said, "because you know you always consider that they're not getting the sort of discipline that you got when you were small, so that is bad enough to start with."

About the Prince of Wales, Princess Anne said: "We live in the same house, at opposite ends of the corridor, but that's roughly speaking all. He usually goes out at different times of the day. But—normally speaking, the normal sort of school holidays, which we stick to because of the two younger brothers. We see quite a lot of each other—and then, roughly speaking, that's enough, quite frankly."

Of clothes and fashions in general, she said: "It is always a total mystery to me why I am described as a fashion leader. Clothes are part of the job—if you can call it a job."

The Princess showed some neat touches of off-the-cuff humour in the film. Photographing giraffe she commented laconically: "They are ideally suited for necking, which they do all the time and don't mind which sex."

Inevitably, riding cropped up as a subject for discussion and the Princess frankly admitted that one of her ambitions was to compete in the Olympics. But she did not think she would have been a riding professional had she not been a Princess. "I think I might have found myself a job, so I would not have had time," she said.

Another film, also made for the Save the Children Fund, and called, *The Princess and the Children* gave some more intriguing and informal glimpses of the Princess. In the film, produced to publicise the fund and its work, the Princess talked with children at an Islington play group. A boy told her he went to football matches and

Moment of relaxation during the European Championships at Burghley . . . Princess Anne talking with Mrs Oliver and Mr Lars Sederholm.

asked her what teams she liked. She said: "I'm not too fussy. I like a lot of clubs—Tottenham, Chelsea. I think Arsenal has got enough supporters."

Speaking about life at Buckingham Palace, Princess Anne told a girl: "It gets quite lonely up there, you know . . . big rooms . . . big corridors . . . you wouldn't like it there, would you?"

A boy piped up: "If there was a big room where you could play football, then I'd like it." Princess Anne replied: "Well, my small brother plays football in the corridors."

On the so-called generation gap, the Princess commented: "It is one of those situations where I think I have had the advantage of knowing both worlds, having grown up in an adult atmosphere at home, and young one at school.

"Personally, I think this gap is very much exaggerated and is more or less used as an excuse for non-communication between age groups."

One bold young man in the film invited the Princess to his club. She asked him what went on there and he replied: "You'll soon find out if you go to the girls' room. There'll be all the boys in there and they start kissing them." "Do they, indeed," said the Princess. "That's what's called the girls' room is it?" The boy added that girls were not allowed in the boys' room because "they always muck around". "Sounds to me," said the Princess, "as if when you go to the girls' room, you do a bit of mucking around."

Newspapers, also have a part to play in offering something of the real "flavour" of a person. While visiting Dusseldorf, Princess Anne told the local Mayor that she thought Britain would "go berserk" if it followed the example of most countries and switched to driving on the right. After mentioning Britain's imminent conversion to decimal currency and the metric system, she added: "They can't possibly change the roads on top of all that or they'll go berserk."

Another newspaper report contained items which came from a booklet privately published by Buckingham Palace for the benefit of those who had to entertain the Princess at official functions. It contained the information that the Princess herself does not smoke, but has no objection to others doing so; that she drinks wine only where toasts are involved, otherwise soft drinks, preferably Coca-Cola; that if the Princess herself speaks, it will be briefly; and that she prefers meals to be reasonably simple.

Despite the necessarily formal and restricted life she is forced to live, Princess Anne has made it clear that she is no recruit for Women's Lib. Speaking at the launching of the Royal Navy frigate *Amazon* at Southampton, she wondered why she had been chosen to launch the ship.

She went on: "I reckon, however, I found the answer in this piece of information pertaining to the Amazons, those formidable forerunners of the Women's Liberation movement—with whom, incidentally, I have no sympathy. They were, apparently, at their most formidable on horseback."

4

Princess Anne was first lifted on to a pony at the tender age of two and a half. This was in 1953 and already by the next summer she was capable of joining the Queen and Prince Charles on rides in the private grounds of Windsor Castle. A year later and she was taken to watch the judging at the Royal Windsor Horse Show, where she saw the Queen's pony William win a highly commended rosette. That same year, the Queen gave permission for the European Horse Trials to be held at Windsor and, with other members of the Royal family, Princess Anne was an excited spectator.

The first appearance of Princess Anne in a public competition came in 1962 when she won a blue rosette on her pony Bandit. A few days earlier she had joined the Garth Hunt Pony Club and turned up unexpectedly for the club's hunter trials at Allanbay Park, Binfield, the home of Major and Mrs John Wills. In her first ride, in the novices under-fourteen class (Princess Anne was only eleven) she came second, winning the blue rosette. She also took part in two other events but was unplaced in either of them.

After this early taste of success, Princess Anne also competed in a local gymkhana held at the Coach Park at Ascot Racecourse in aid of the building fund of a local Roman Catholic church. With her mother and father watching, Princess Anne competed in six events, taking fourth prize in the class for working horses. The Queen and Prince Philip also saw their daughter compete in the jumping class for riders under eighteen where she had one clear round but was eliminated in the first jump off.

Obviously the Princess must have enjoyed her initiation into the world of competitive riding because a few days later she and her brother, with the aid of the Crown Equerry, Lt-Col John Miller, organised a pony gymkhana of their own in Home Park, Windsor Castle. A special jumping course was laid out near the East Terrace and some twenty children were invited to take part. The show was completely private and special precautions were taken to prevent gatecrashers. The main jumping event was won by the eleven-year-old Princess but the best her brother could manage was eighth place out of fifteen competitors.

Schooldays at Benenden then intervened but the new schoolgirl could still find opportunities to follow her favourite pastime. Towards the end of her first year at the school she was chosen to be one of the Benenden show-jumping team to compete against Bedgebury Park and Lillesden, two neighbouring schools. The Princess rode High Jinks, the pony she had already ridden to several prizes and awards. On this occasion she won two prizes, a red rosette as a member of the team which won the junior combined training cup, and a yellow rosette for being third equal in the under-fourteen section of the dressage challenge cup.

Princess Anne was rapidly developing into a bold, determined rider—and perhaps inevitably, she soon suffered her first minor accident. In December, 1964, she cracked a bone in the little finger of her right hand when she caught the hand in her horse's reins while out riding from Benenden. She was taken to the Beaumont House Nursing Home in Beaumont Street, Marylebone, where she was given an anaesthetic while a minor operation was carried out.

The injury quickly healed and in the following April she made her first competitive appearance at the Badminton Horse Trials. On the eight-year-old brown High Jinks she was placed first in the class for novice children's working ponies. The Princess, whose entry came as a surprise as she was not mentioned in the programme, rode a clear round over seven fences against nineteen other young competitors.

There was no doubt that by this time Princess Anne was dedicated to her hobby. At every opportunity she was practising, practising, practising. When staying at Windsor she took the faithful High Jinks over a special course laid out in the private grounds of Home Park.

On April 21, 1965, the Queen's birthday, Princess Anne took home a special present for her mother in the shape of a red rosette won for a faultless and confident display of horsemanship at the Garth Hunt Pony Club's hunter trials held at the 300-acre Cruchfield Manor Farm, near Warfield in Berkshire. She shared first place with two other girls out of twenty competitors. The judges at the trials were watching for style and approach to the jumps and it was a measure of the Princess's rapid improvement and general confidence that she came through without incurring any penalty points.

Without doubt, one of the principal reasons for the continued success of British riders in the Three-Day Event comes from the opportunities for training which they enjoy while out hunting. But because of the passions aroused by the sport, this particular form of training is barred to the Princess. As early as March, 1955—when the Princess was still only four—the National Society for the Abolition of Cruel Sports made their feelings plain in a letter to the Queen asking that the Royal children should not be required to submit to the "barbarous and revolting" custom of "blooding" at a fox hunt. A custom, incidentally, which has largely died out now.

Fortunately, there is a perfectly acceptable alternative to hunting which also provides excellent training for eventing. This comes from following draghounds. In dragging, hounds follow a scent, usually put down by dragging a cloth soaked in aniseed across hunting country.

But in dragging, as in riding in general, the slightest error can sometimes be severely punished, as Princess Anne discovered to her cost when she was thrown and broke her nose while out with the Oxford University Draghounds at Shotover Park, Oxfordshire.

Describing the incident, the master of the Draghounds said: "About twenty of us were riding across boggy farmland. Princess Anne's horse, which must have been tired, fell at the last fence—a hedge with a rail on top. The Princess seemed shaken but no more so than anyone would be after a fall like that. She was taken back to the house but I had no idea until later that she had been injured." An operation to straighten Princess Anne's nose was carried out at the King Edward VII Hospital for Officers.

5

With Princess Anne's interest in equestrianism firmly established, the decision was taken early in 1968 that she should receive more advanced coaching. Lt-Col John Miller, the Crown Equerry, whose special responsibility it is to look after the Queen's horses, made the initial approach to Mrs Alison Oliver at her Warfield Training Stables. At first, no mention was made of coaching Princess Anne, Mrs Oliver merely being asked if she would school on a horse for the Princess. At this time, of course, Princess Anne was still a pupil at Benenden but when holiday time came around she began spending more and more time at Warfield—and coaching by Mrs Oliver just followed naturally.

Alison Oliver was not born into the so-called "horsey" set—in fact, no one else in her family had ever been really interested in riding. She lived her early years in Lancashire, near Southport, had her first riding lesson at the age of seven—and was immediately and completely enamoured of the sport. Every day, she would visit the stables and when she left school she worked first at stables near Ormskirk and later with Mr Lars Sederholm, who has trained, among others, Richard Walker, the 1969 Badminton winner. As Alison Coulton, she competed in many trials and after her marriage to Alan Oliver, the show-jumping champion, she continued in top events, including the three-day world championships. But she admits herself that since she started training Princess Anne her own interest in competing has fallen-off. "If I am riding myself, then I want to think only of my worries, not anyone else's," she says. So now she prefers to keep her mind wholly on Princess Anne.

It was quite early in their association—in August, 1968, in fact, just a few months after Mrs Oliver had taken on the training job—that Princess Anne first entered the hurly-burly of the one-day event. Riding her own gelding Purple Star, she took part in the tough Eridge Horse Trials in Sussex, in a novice event for riders under twenty-one. Asked at the time about the Princess's chances, Mrs Oliver cautiously remarked: "As things have gone so far she has done very well indeed. But I don't know whether it would be possible for her to develop into a rider of international class."

In fact, Princess Anne finished fifth of about thirty young riders in the combined event. She delayed her turn in the dressage, waiting for the Queen to arrive to watch her, and then rode confidently, finishing the section with 31 penalty points and in seventh place. Purple Star refused at a double fence in the show-jumping but cleared it at the second attempt. Princess Anne had three time penalties in the cross-country.

Gradually the Princess continued to gain in confidence and in October, 1968, she appeared before an audience of thousands at the Horse of the Year Show at Wembley. Dressed as a Georgian nobleman, she was one of a team of four from the Battle and District Riding Club, Sussex, competing in the quadrille dressage finals. It was at Wembley that Princess Anne first told friends that she intended to compete in a full programme of show-jumping and three-day event competitions during the following year, now that her schooldays were behind her.

What exactly was this three-day event in which the Princess was so interested? The Combined Training Committee of the British Horse Society, the ruling body of the sport, describe it as a comprehensive test of both horse and rider. The rider must be able to train and condition the horse in order to produce his best performance; and the horse, in turn, must be fit, supple and obedient, possessing both stamina and speed.

In the three-day event the same horse and rider have to undergo three distinct tests, on, if possible, three consecutive days. (Actually, with the great upsurge of interest in the sport and consequent increase in numbers entering, this is not always possible. In championships and other major three-day events, the dressage is now almost invariably run on two days.) The dressage consists of a series of exercises designed to test the horse's training and obedience. Penalty points are marked by a panel of judges. The most testing part of the three-day event—and certainly the most exciting—comes in the speed, endurance and cross-country section. This takes place over a 13-25 miles route, partly along roads and tracks, partly over a steeplechase course and partly across country, with fixed, natural obstacles. The course has to be completed within a fixed time, penalties being incurred for falls and disobedience at the obstacles. After this gruelling section, a veterinary examination takes place and if the horse passes he then takes part in the jumping section, which is designed simply to prove that despite the great demands made upon him, he remains fit and supple.

Interest in the sport has grown steadily each year and in order to prepare horses and riders for the major annual events, the British Horse Society instituted similar competitions on a smaller scale, known as horse trials. Like the three-day event, these comprise dressage, cross-country and jumping tests—but the cross-country course is much shorter and the whole competition can be completed in one day. The official grades of horse trials are Novice, Intermediate, open-Intermediate and Advanced, so a competitor may proceed by careful stages from simple competitions as a novice to the full-scale three-day event.

Commenting on the Princess's decision to compete in a full programme, Colonel "Babe" Molesey, who was then chairman of the Olympic Three-Day Event Selection Committee, said: "There is absolutely no reason why she shouldn't represent her country one day. It all depends on the horse. She has been well taught but her present horse is only a novice. Even so, she has done extremely well. Obviously we welcome her interest in the sport. As in the past, she will be treated exactly as any other competitor."

Whenever she is staying at Windsor or Buckingham Palace, and her official duties permit, Princess Anne visits Mrs Oliver's stables daily. Her four horses—Purple Star, Doublet, Collingwood and Columbus—are all kept there. Doublet, Collingwood and Columbus were all bred by the Queen and Purple Star was bred by Colonel Miller, who gave the gelding to the Princess.

Colonel Miller, who was in the Welsh Guards for twenty-two years and gives his recreations as hunting, shooting, polo and driving, has obviously played a considerable part in the development of Princess Anne as a competent horsewoman. He became Crown Equerry in 1961 and there were some rumbles of discontent soon after his appointment by Mews Staff who complained that excessive regimentation and parades were more suitable for soldiers than civilians. What many might think the complete answer to these grumbles was given by the Colonel's former adjutant who said of the "spit and polish" allegation: "I was his adjutant for two years and would only say that, if anything, he was more liberal than his predecessors in this respect. Of course, he has high standards and these civilians at the Palace are not Guardsmen. But after all, they *are* in attendance on the Queen." No more grumbles were heard. . . .

Incidentally, there is one amusing story about Colonel Miller which has, no doubt, been told and retold with relish in the mess. There can have been few occasions when a senior officer of the Brigade of Guards, without in any way losing his dignity, can have stood for several minutes in full view of the battalion he used to command clutching a woman's handbag! But that was what happened to Colonel Miller in the garden at Buckingham Palace when the Queen presented new colours to the 1st Battalion, Welsh Guards to mark their fiftieth anniversary. Before

The start of the 1971 season and
Princess Anne, with her personal
detective, Mr David Coleman, walks the
course at the Crookham Trials.

*Conversation piece at Crookham—with
Princess Anne pointing to the spot where it
happened. . . .*

The lonely slog of the dedicated competitor—
the part the spectator rarely sees. . . .
Princess Anne walks round the cross-country
course at Badminton in 1971 in the early
morning before competition begins.

The obstacle looks formidable—but close behind, ready to offer advice, is Mrs Oliver.

Mrs Oliver tells the Princess how she should tackle it. . . .

On now to the next problem. . . .

Pause for thought and more discussion.

Relaxing now near the
end of the inspection, with
the discreet Mr Coleman
coming into the picture.

The cross-country—and at the
water it's a case of in . . .

. . . through . . .

. . . and out again!

The Queen waits anxiously for her daughter's return in the cross-country.

Where is Princess Anne? The Queen is joined in her vigil by Princess Margaret.

Still waiting. . . but now with the Queen Mother.

Tense. . . alert. . . Princess Anne and Doublet at Eridge in 1971.

Meanwhile. . . Princess Anne concentrates hard as she prepares to take a downhill triple bar.

Over the Whitbread bar. . .

. . . and safely past the finishing line at the end of the cross–country section.

Eridge Park and a look round with Mrs. Oliver.

Conditions in the cross-country were described as "challenging" —with the going "fairly sticky".

Princess Anne completes one of only 10 clear rounds in the cross-country.

A first chance to talk over her clear round with Mrs Oliver.

Safely over this one at Crookham.

Explaining to Mrs Oliver that at Fence 18 Doublet had his only refusal. It was an expensive mistake because, brought in again, he straddled the fence, Princess Anne slipped from the saddle— the penalty points plummeting her from first place to 12th.

A burdened Princess Anne makes for the weigh-in after completing the cross-country section at Eridge.

beginning her speech, the Queen took her notes from Colonel Miller and handed him her bag until she had finished. . . .

Doublet, of course, as an open horse, is the one that Princess Anne will ride in Munich if she is chosen for the Olympic Games. According to Mrs Oliver he is a magnificent horse, brave and obedient. Also, he has the happy knack of appearing perfectly at home whatever the conditions might be. For example, there can rarely have been a greater contrast than there was between the going at the 1971 Badminton event and the European Championships at Burghley five months later. At Badminton continuous, drenching rain made the going very heavy, sticky and treacherous—while at Burghley, during an Indian summer, despite rain on the second day, the going was distinctly good to hard. Yet Doublet coped perfectly on both occasions.

During her time as a regular competitor at three-day events, Mrs Oliver was a renowned dressage rider. It is obviously more than coincidence, therefore, that Princess Anne always does exceedingly well in the dressage and frequently leads the field.

Purple Star has been the ideal horse for bringing Princess Anne along through the lesser events since her Pony Club days. And in Collingwood and Columbus, full brothers and bred by the Queen, she has two immensely promising intermediate horses.

Even during tours abroad about her Royal business, Princess Anne has, somehow or other, contrived to increase and improve her riding experience. For example, it so happened that her first official visit abroad was to Austria, with the Queen and Prince Philip, in May, 1969. Unfortunately, Princess Anne was laid low by a bout of influenza just before they were due to leave and her parents had to travel without her. The Princess made a quick recovery, however, joining the Queen and Prince Philip two days later in Vienna, where one of her first engagements was a visit to the world famous Spanish Riding School. Here she took with both hands the chance to ride one of the magnificent Lipizzaner horses. Wearing a black coat, light-coloured breeches and black boots, and with her hair straggling out of its pony tail, she rode round the ring at the school on a thirteen-year-old stallion belonging to Colonel Hans Handler, head of the school. After watching a quarter-of-an-hour's performance, carried out, incidentally, in front of photographers from the world's Press, the Colonel was full of admiration. "You can see what a good horsewoman she is," he said. "I was amazed when she did one of the intricate movements."

Experts, then, even of Colonel Handler's standing were in full agreement over the Princess's ability and exciting potential as a rider. But still she needed more experience, more competition—and with Mrs Oliver to guide and advise her she continued competing at tougher and tougher events. But it was not until the Princess's operation in the middle of 1971 that Mrs Oliver realised that she might have a future champion on her hands.

The strain of competition
howing at Eridge.

Recalling her visit to Princess Anne in the King Edward VII Hospital for Officers just after the operation, Mrs Oliver says it was then that she realised again that the Princess had the steely determination to reach the top.

"When I first saw her ride, I could see she was a good, competent horsewoman—but I don't think anyone could have said then, 'Yes, she is international material'," says Mrs Oliver. "As I got to know her better, during her visits to my stables, I began to realise just how enthusiastic she was. But when I walked into that hospital room, I knew then that the determination was also there.

"When I had first heard about the operation, I must admit that I had thought, 'Well, that's it.' Princess Anne needed to ride at Eridge (the final trial before the European Championships) but it was due to take place so soon after the operation that I thought there was no hope. Princess Anne might easily have said, when I saw her in hospital, 'Oh dear. Poor me—isn't it terrible? This has ruined everything.' Instead, there she was, sitting in a chair making plans for her crash keep-fit course. She had it all worked out that she would go to Balmoral to convalesce, so that she could do lots of walking and climbing in order to be able to ride at Eridge.

"When we got to Eridge, I thought she might have to skip the roads and tracks and steeplechase. But when I saw how well she was going, I advised her to complete the full event. It was obviously the best thing for both her and Doublet."

6

At the beginning of 1971, it was by no means certain that Princess Anne would be invited to compete in the European Championships at Burghley. A lot of good riders were in contention for places, and with 1971 being pre-Olympic year, every trial took on added importance.

The Royal rider started the season well with a polished dressage test and clear round in the Crookham Trials at the end of March. A few days later she beat a whole number of more experienced horses and riders to take fourth place in the Midland Bank Open-Intermediate class at Rushall Horse Trials, the event being won in superb manner by Lt Mark Phillips on Great Ovation. A lot of imagination had been shown in arranging the cross-country at Rushall and there were far fewer clear rounds than usual. Doublet had been given to Princess Anne by the Queen at the beginning of 1971 and, riding with zest and enthusiasm, the Princess showed the right proportions of dash and discretion to earn the applause of the experts.

Then came the Badminton Three-Day Event on the Duke of Beaufort's estate in Gloucestershire, where it was vital to do well as the invitations for Burghley would follow. Success at Badminton in any year confers the blue riband of three-day competitions—in pre-Olympic year, its importance could not be over-stressed. Badminton was the very first open three-day event the Princess and Doublet had ever tackled, previously Princess Anne's combined experience having been restricted to the one-day horse trials and a standard three-day event on Purple Star at Tidworth.

As Mrs Oliver says, the thing with three-day eventing is that until horse and rider actually try it, they have no idea what might happen—in spite of whatever training they may have done beforehand. So the Princess and Doublet travelled to Gloucestershire without any exaggerated hopes, but with the greatest determination to do their best in the classic event. And, once again, Princess Anne made her customary good start, leading with Doublet after twenty-five of the fifty-one declared starters had completed their dressage on the first day.

Riding with precision and admirable composure and concentration, Princess Anne amassed only 82.5 penalty points—five in front of second-placed Anne Morrell on Sandpiper IV. Despite the attention her performance had aroused from the watching crowds—to say nothing of the television cameras—Princess Anne at that stage was already ahead of one past Badminton winner, Richard Walker, who was lying equal third on Upper Strata with 94.01 points. On the same mark was the top overseas competitor, Ireland's Simon Walford with Chester. James Templer, the Olympic rider, on Off Centre was fifth with 95.51.

But waiting in the wings were plenty of other top-class competitors, including Mary Gordon-Watson, then the World and European Champion, with Cornishman V, and Derek Allhusen and Lochinvar, winners of gold and silver medals in Mexico. They had missed the previous year's Badminton because Major Allhusen had broken his leg before the season started—and were, therefore, even more determined than ever to do well. The overseas challenge, in addition to the Irish, came from Sweden, Switzerland and Holland. This, then, was the measure of the opposition facing Princess Anne.

In the midst of great excitement, the dressage phase was duly completed the next day—and only one pair, Mark Phillips and his eight-year-old Great Ovation, with 75.5 penalty points, managed to get in front of Princess Anne. Lt Phillips, of the 1st Queen's Dragoon Guards, was reserve rider for the Mexico gold medal team and a member of the team which had won the world championship. On that occasion Lt Phillips had ridden Chicago, later sold to Germany, but he had made steady progress with Great Ovation, a son of the Cesarewitch winner, Three Cheers.

Lying third behind Princess Anne after the dressage was Sweden's national champion, Sgt Jan Jonsson, on Sarajevo, with 86 points. Run throughout in rain, the second part of the dressage was not, in general, superior to the first day's as had been expected, and Anne Morrell's Sandpiper IV was still fourth. The favourites, Mary Gordon-Watson and Cornishman V were fifth with 88.5 points, one and a half points ahead of Major Allhusen and Lochinvar. But with less than fifteen points covering the first six, the event was clearly wide open.

The decisive and most vital section of all in three-day eventing is the cross-country. Many good riders will take the most fearsome fences without a second thought in the heat of the hunt, but they will think twice about tackling similar big fences on their own, in cold blood—as the event competitor must do. Badminton has what many experienced riders regard as one of the most rigorous cross-country courses in the world. The sorting-out process was about to begin. . . .

Torrential rain all the previous night had made conditions very challenging and Princess Anne and Doublet jumped one of the only ten clear rounds that day. By keeping up a spanking pace, they ended in fourth place. Still ahead of the field after a great gallop in the cross-country were Lt Phillips and Great Ovation, clearly determined to hang on to their advantage. Miss Gordon-Watson and Cornishman V jumped all the big fences with their characteristic style and grace but came unstuck at the Coffin, where they got too close to the final rail. Cornishman had to stop—and that meant they had to be content with second place, 20 points behind the leader. The distinction of having the fastest time of the day went to Richard Walker and Upper Strata, who took third place despite misjudging the approach to a fence and incurring a technical refusal.

So to the final day of Badminton 1971, and the show-jumping section. And Lt Mark Phillips and Great Ovation put their final seal of authority on the whole event by completing their start-to-finish triumph in masterly style with more than two fences in hand over Mary Gordon-Watson and Cornishman V.

Lt Phillips, twenty-two, had been given leave from his regiment to prepare for Badminton and his victory bore no semblance of a fluke. Yet only six months earlier, so little was thought of Great Ovation's potential, that serious consideration was given to selling him. But during the winter, Lt Phillips hunted him and the transformation began. He took Great Ovation in hunter trials during the spring and got the feel of a much more determined horse, but even so was not sure whether Great Ovation had sufficient experience for Badminton. Probably if Lt Phillips had known how wet and sticky the going was to become, the horse would not have been started—but he jumped clear both in the steeplechase and the cross-country and came into the final show-jumping phase still well in command. When Miss Gordon-Watson and Cornishman V faulted out at the eighth of the show-jumping fences, Great Ovation was left able to have two fences down and still win. But so immaculately did he jump that he did not need even one.

And what of Princess Anne and Doublet, competing, remember, in their very first Badminton three-day event? Well, with just one show-jumping error after their most severe trial to date, Princess Anne and Doublet took fifth place—a "highly satisfactory" outcome, as Mrs Oliver said later.

So, the final results at Badminton, 1971, for the Whitbread Trophy, were: 1st—Lt M. Phillips's Great Ovation, 125.9 penalty points; 2nd—Miss M. Gordon-Watson's Cornishman V, 155.7; 3rd—Miss Deborah West's Baccarat, 158.9; 4th—Mr and Mrs Compton-Bracebridge's Upper Strata (Richard Walker) 159.61; 5th—Princess Anne's Doublet 166.9; and 6th—Michael Tucker's Farmer Giles, 167.9.

For her fifth position at Badminton, Princess Anne won a prize of £150—but far more important to her was the announcement that came a few days later. Although left out of the official team short-list, she was invited to compete as an individual in the European Three-Day Event Championships at Burghley in September. This meant, of course, that Princess Anne and Doublet could be in line for the individual title, as happened with Mary Gordon-Watson and Cornishman V in 1969.

In announcing the short-list of eight for the team, the selectors said that they had been "greatly impressed" by Princess Anne's performance on Doublet at Badminton. At the same time, they took into account that this was the first international for both horse and rider and that there were a lot of riders with considerable international experience.

Knowledgeable observers agreed at the time that this compromise by the selectors was an eminently sensible one, for had Princess Anne been selected for the team the pressure on her at that stage in her riding career would have been considerable.

7

There can be few pleasanter places to be in September, at the start of a long Indian summer, than Burghley Park, situated on the Northamptonshire—Lincolnshire border near the heart of England's hunting country. Built by the First Lord Burghley, who was Lord High Treasurer to Queen Elizabeth I, Burghley is generally acknowledged as being the largest and grandest house of the first Elizabethan age. Built round the remains of a twelfth-century monastery, the mansion—some would say palace—has some 240 rooms filled with rare and valuable furniture and historic relics. The Great Hall in the oldest part of the house is 68 feet long and 60 feet high, with a magnificent hammer-beam roof. The Heaven Room is so called because its walls and ceiling have been painted to create the illusion that the visitor is standing among the clouds. In fact, it is generally considered to be the finest painted room in Europe. The Sixth Marquess of Exeter, who as Lord Burghley was himself an Olympic Gold Medallist, now lives in the house, which is open to the public in Spring, Summer and Autumn. The wonderful deer park was landscaped by the prolific Capability Brown—and all this formed the setting for the 1971 European Three-Day Event Championship.

Great Britain came to the event as firm favourites—for they were unbeaten in the previous four seasons, having won the European titles in 1967 and 1969, the

Olympic Gold in 1968 and the World Championship in Punchestown in 1970. But there was great disappointment in the British camp when Richard Walker, who had been runner-up in the previous European Three-Day Event Championship at Haras du Pin had to forgo the chance to go one better when Upper Strata, the Australian-bred nine-year-old was found to be lame and had to be withdrawn a day before the championship started. As a result Debbie West's Baccarat, who looked to have missed his chance when the team's other invalid, The Poacher, was passed fit, received promotion from the reserve ranks. The full British team then was: Mary Gordon-Watson and Cornishman V, the reigning World and European Champions, Mark Phillips, with Great Ovation, Richard Meade, with The Poacher, and Miss West, with Baccarat.

Despite the all-round strength of the British riders, they knew they would face plenty of stiff opposition from the Italians, Russians, Irish, Swiss and West Germans. The Italians, who had caused something of a major upset by winning the Gold at the Tokyo Olympics, sent two of their Tokyo team, Paolo Angioni and Allessandro Argenton. The Russians had made an incredible overland journey to the championships but very sensibly had given themselves plenty of time to acclimatise their new horses.

In recent years, the Burghley Three-Day Event has tended to be overshadowed to some extent by the proximity of other major competitions—but this was certainly not the case in 1971 when the best riders and horses in Europe were assembled to do battle. The scene in magnificent Burghley Park was all set for a great contest—and it was certain that whoever won the team and individual prizes would be worthy champions indeed.

Although they had been left out of the official British team, Princess Anne and Doublet had an excellent example to follow in that set by Miss Gordon-Watson in 1969. She, too, had competed as an "invited individual", and not as a member of the British team, and had gone on to win the individual title.

In the spring, Princess Anne and Doublet had gone into the Badminton event as unknown quantities. As Mrs Oliver had said—until they had actually competed in a Three-Day classic, no one could possibly tell what might happen. Before Badminton, therefore, Mrs Oliver had been unable to judge what the outcome might be. It was a different matter at Burghley now that she knew the strength of Princess Anne and Doublet. She could look at the list of competitors—or, at least at those competitors she had seen ride before—and make a shrewd estimate of their chances. Later Mrs Oliver was to admit that having run the rule over the opposition she thought to herself, "Well, if the Princess and Doublet are both fit, they can win here—so long as their luck is in."

Mrs Oliver's husband, Alan, who has had vast experience of competitive riding at all levels and whose skill and daring on the legendary Red Admiral, now, alas, dead, thrilled millions of television viewers, has strong views on the importance of luck in all sporting events—and certainly in the equestrian world. As he says, the rider may come out feeling on top of the world, absolutely fighting fit—but he has no way of knowing if his horse is in the same mood. Mr Oliver cites the Mexico Olympic Three-Day Event as a perfect example of the importance luck or circumstances can play in equestrianism. The cross-country course in Mexico was big, even tough—but strictly fair. But just before the finals, torrential rain flooded the course, turning the tough, fair test into a virtual killer. Horses had to plough their way through mud—it was the sort of thing no one could have planned for. But, as luck would have it, the British found they could cope best with these fantastic conditions—and the team gold medal was their reward. All you can do in any equestrian event, says Mr Oliver, is to have yourself and your horse as fit as possible—then keep your fingers crossed!

Before and during the European championships, Mrs Oliver and her Royal pupil were out early every morning, sizing-up the course, checking the formidable obstacles. "It was very interesting to see the competitors from other countries eyeing Princess Anne and wondering, perhaps, whether she was really good enough to be in such exalted company," says Mrs Oliver. The Russians, as one might have expected, were particularly intrigued. One morning when Mrs Oliver and the Princess were out early they twice passed the Russians—and on each occasion Mrs Oliver thought the Russians were going to speak. But each time they went on without saying a word. But the third time they met, some members of the Russian party plucked up courage and hesitantly greeted the Princess. They were obviously delighted when she responded with a pleasant, "Good morning". In fact, at the end of the championships, just before they left for home, the five Russian riders revealed that they thought the Princess was "an excellent rider and a wonderful girl". As a tangible mark of their regard, they asked Mr Yuri Darakhvelidze, a Russian sportswriter, to present the Princess with a bronze souvenir medal on their behalf.

Because of the numbers competing in the championships, the dressage at Burghley had to be spread over two days, with Princess Anne and Doublet drawn to complete their section on the opening day. The weather was ideal and the going was just about perfect. From the moment that Princess Anne rode into the ring and gravely saluted the judges, it was obvious that she and Doublet were about to present something special. This, indeed, proved to be the case, for moving with fluency and freedom, they performed a smooth test, amassing only 41.5 penalty points, putting them well ahead of the Swiss Captain Paul Heurlimann and Grand Times on 52.5. Lying third after this first day was the experienced French horse Quolibet, who was in the team that finished second in the World Championships at Punchestown in 1970, ridden on this occasion by Jean-Luc Cornille. The eleven year-old finished nine points behind Grand Times.

Just one point behind them came the best of the British official team, Debbie West, with Baccarat who, despite being promoted only at the last moment, went round with considerable confidence to stand one point ahead of Russia's Anatoli Shebanov, an equestrian trainer from Moscow, on Afin. The then reigning individual champion, Mary Gordon-Watson, with Cornishman V, was lying sixth with 71 penalties—but it was known that the cross-country was their main strength.

The leaders in the dressage after the first day were: Princess Anne's Doublet 41.5 penalty points, 1; Capt. P. Heurlimann's Grand Times (Switzerland) 52.5, 2; J.-L. Cornille's Quolibet (France) 61.5, 3; Miss D. West's Baccarat 62.5, 4.

Luck played its first major part in the championships on the next day, which was set aside for the completion of the dressage section. The pleasant, warm sunshine of the opening day turning to almost perpetual rain. And Princess Anne, safely home and dry so far as the dressage was concerned, held on to her lead at the head of the individual classification. The British, too, eased into a narrow lead in the team event—and in both cases the nearest challenge came from the Russians. Their team score, counting all four members, although at the final reckoning only the best three would count, was 278.5 points to Great Britain's 259, with Switzerland right on their heels with 281.

Doublet's dressage score of 41.5 penalty points ridden, admittedly, in very much more pleasant conditions, began to look really useful, only Russia's Sergei Mukhin, at twenty one of the youngest riders competing, being able to better 50 penalties. On the seven-year-old stallion Resfeder he gave Russia a much-needed boost, going last, with a most accomplished test for 49 penalties. The Russians, furnished with young horses—one eight-year-old and three at seven—were beginning to look dangerous.

The experienced French horse Quaker, ridden by Michel Cochenet, who had finished eighth in the previous year's world championships, was lying third on 52, just half a point ahead of Captain Heurlimann and Grand Times. Richard Meade on The Poacher, who as so often before had to perform his dressage in the worst of the weather, came out best of the official British team with 59 points—and was thought unlucky by many to have received so many. Debbie West and Baccarat were thus next best on 62.5, two ahead of Mark Phillips and Great Ovation, with the reigning champions, Mary Gordon-Watson and Cornishman V unexpectedly providing the discard of 71, which left them in fifteenth place individually.

With the dressage finally completed, the individual leaders were: Princess Anne's Doublet, 41.5, 1; S. Mukhin's Resfeder (Russia) 49, 2; M. Cochenet's Quaker (France) 52, 3; Capt. P. Heurlimann's Grand Times (Switzerland) 52.5, 4. In the team event, the position was: Great Britain 257, 1; Russia 278.5, 2; Switzerland 281, 3; France 304, 4.

The dressage, however, slipped into its appropriately insignificant place when compared with the roads and tracks, steeplechase and the cross-country, which took place the next day. The cross-country course, which was nearly five miles long, was obviously going to make considerable demands on both horse and rider. It was eminently fair, but, as was demanded by an event of this stature, it clearly asked some stiff questions. A number of entirely new fences had been included by the course builder and for tiring horses, the big fences near the end were to take a severe toll. The "preliminaries", it might be said, were over and the real examination of skill, courage and determination of both horse and rider was about to begin.

And Princess Anne, riding with great dash, determination and confidence, became one of only nine riders to complete this stiff course without a stop or a fall. Indeed, with a score of only 60.3 penalties, she lengthened her lead and was 28 points ahead of the first British team member, Debbie West on Baccarat, with world champion Mary Gordon-Watson, on Cornishman V, in third place, another nine points behind.

With Doublet responding gallantly to every demand made on him, Princess Anne attacked the cross-country fences like a veteran. They had no serious problems, although Doublet had a little difficulty in getting out of the Trout Hatchery. Several horses and riders had already taken a ducking there before Princess Anne and Doublet arrived. For a moment, Doublet "lost" a front leg, but his rider gave him his head, letting the reins run free, and Doublet picked up without mishap. At the same spot, Richard Meade and The Poacher had a stop. Princess Anne's time was several seconds faster than any member of the official British team.

Perhaps it was not surprising that on their home ground, British horses coped best with the testing course, which the foreign visitors found very difficult. So much so that at the end of the day the British team were 425 points ahead of the French, with Ireland, Russia and Italy, close on the French heels. Holland and Switzerland were eliminated.

With the second and most important section completed, the leaders were: Princess Anne's Doublet, dressage 41.5, steeplechase 0, cross-country 18.8, total 60.3, 1; Miss D. West's Baccarat, 62.5, 0, 25.6—88.1, 2; Miss M. Gordon-Watson's Cornishman V, 71, 0, 26—97.3, 3; Mr S. Stevens's Classic Chips, 98.5, 0, 4.4—102.9, 4; Mr R. Meade's The Poacher, 59, 0, 49.2—108.25, 5; Miss J. Hodgson's Larkspur, 84.5, 0, 31—115.7, 6; Lt M. Phillips's Great Ovation, 64.5, 0, 52.4—116.9, 7. The team position with one day to go, was: Great Britain 293.3, 1; France 718.9, 2; Ireland 724.1, 3; Russia 745.5, 4; Italy 808.9, 5. Incidentally, it is interesting to note that Stewart Stevens, on Classic Chips—like Princess Anne a British individual entry—owed his sudden high placing in the ratings to an absolutely storming round in the cross-country, in which he returned by far the fastest time to overcome a modest dressage score.

Before the last day's show-jumping phase, there was the veterinary examination to be passed, to ensure that the horses had not injured themselves in the cross-country section. Here the French suffered severely when Michel Cochenet's Quaker had to be withdrawn with a badly swollen knee, which meant that the score of their fourth horse had to be counted, adding enough penalties so that they lost their second place.

One day to go then, with only the show-jumping left, and who could blame Mrs Oliver for now thinking thoughts of victory—although she dare not say as much to her Royal pupil. She had been afraid even to dwell on the possibility until the cross-country course had been safely negotiated but with Princess Anne and Doublet able to have two fences down and still win, Mrs Oliver was now confident that success was well within their grasp.

There was an enormous crowd gathered around the big jumping arena at Burghley as Princess Anne rode Doublet into the enclosure and saluted her mother and father, who had come to see her put the final seal on her triumph. She appeared completely calm and unhurried and obviously had Doublet beautifully collected as they sailed over fence after fence for a perfect, faultless round.

So Princess Anne and Doublet completed, with a flourish, their start-to-finish triumph. In doing so they led a rout of competitors from nine countries, British riders filling the first eight places in the individual classification.

The British team beat the Russians with more than 400 points to spare to complete their fifth consecutive success in Olympic, World and Continental championships.

The show-jumping course, which, in truth, was fairly innocuous, had little effect upon the final placings apart from a shuffling of the British. Largely because of the French misfortune with Quaker, the Russians slipped into second place—so, having apparently been told to return with no worse than a bronze, the Russians, in fact, returned home in some triumph with a silver medal.

The final individual placings for the 1971 European Three-Day Event Championship were: Princess Anne's Doublet 60.3 penalty points, 1; Miss D. West's Baccarat 98.1, 2; Mr S. Stevens's Classic Chips 112.9, 3; Miss M. Gordon-Watson's Cornishman V 117, 4; Mr R. Meade's The Poacher 118.2, 5; Lt M. Phillips's Great Ovation 126.9, 6; Miss J. Hodgson's Larkspur 135.7, 7; Miss A. Sowden's Mooncoin 136, 8; Lt Buehler's Wukaris (Switzerland) 143.9, 9; Mr S. Mukhin's Resfeder (Russia) 160.6, 10.

The team championship ended: Great Britain 333.13, 1; Russia 755.5, 2; Ireland 795.6, 3; Italy 848.9, 4; France 949.2, 5.

Thus the championships came to a close, with a fairy-tale ending featuring a real, live Princess. There was one more tiny piece of history to be made. The championship presentations were made by Princess Anne's mother and father, so she became the first European Champion to be kissed by the Queen and Prince Philip.

Afterwards, Princess Anne confessed that she had not really enjoyed herself until it was all over. But with the pressure on her from something like 50,000 spectators, all willing her to do well, perhaps that was not too surprising. Princess Anne, who had to contend with the additional hazard of a low-flying aircraft while tackling the twelve fence show-jumping course, said that she had had no particular worries in the cross-country, despite the hard knock Doublet took. She confessed that she had not been as fit as she might have been, although she had exercised a good deal since her operation, even when cruising in the Royal yacht Britannia. Perhaps it is needless to add, that by her victory, Princess Anne became the first member of the Royal Family ever to hold a European equestrian title.

Her achievements in 1971 brought Princess Anne three more titles and these all came to her, as it were, by popular acclaim. She was voted Sportswoman of the Year by the British Sportswriters' Association; Sportswoman of the Year by readers of the *Daily Express*: and Sports Personality of the Year by BBC television viewers. In the Sportswriters' poll, Princess Anne gained 360 votes, 123 ahead of the next most popular choice, Anne Moore, the world show-jumping champion. Voting was on the basis of who had done most to enhance British sporting prestige internationally. In the *Daily Express* poll, the Princess swept home with more than 51 per cent of the votes cast. Again, Anne Moore was second. And in the BBC television contest, Princess Anne pulled in 4,000 votes more than the runner-up, George Best.

8

Of all the sports open to women in the Olympic Games, one of the toughest must surely be the Three-Day Event. For one thing, the women compete on equal terms with the men, and for another the competition is stretched over three or four days of intense and at times dangerous endeavour. To begin with, the Three-Day Event competitors must control their own nerves so that they can bring out the best from their horses in the dressage test—while all the time lynx-eyed judges are watching every move and awarding penalty points for each and every mistake or omission. Then comes the test of bravery in taking their horses over a cross-country course with the sort of obstacles any sensible man or woman would normally ride miles to avoid. And, finally, the competitors must strive for a clear round in the show-jumping arena, with thousands of spectators' eyes upon them. Yet, incredibly enough, two of the major Three-Day Event titles are currently held by women—Mary Gordon-Watson holding the world crown and Princess Anne the European.

Equestrian events, in the form of show-jumping, were first introduced into the Olympic Games in Paris in 1900. There was polo in 1908 and the first Three-Day Event was held in the 1912 Games in Stockholm. A British team of four started—but none of them finished. Three of them also constituted the show-jumping team and, incidentally, two of the event team, Paul Kenna and Bryan Lawrence later went on to win Victoria Crosses.

In Stockholm in 1912 the host country took both the team and individual titles, Lt Nordlander on Lady Artist winning the individual gold medal. Eight years later in Antwerp, it was again Sweden first and the rest nowhere, the individual gold being taken on this occasion by Count Moerner on Germania.

It was the turn of the Dutch to sweep the board in Paris in 1924, with Lt Voort van Zijp taking the individual gold on the inappropriately named, Silver Piece. The Dutch remained in the ascendancy on their home territory at the 1928 Games in Amsterdam, the individual crown being taken by Lt de Mortanges on Marcroix. Four years later, however, in Los Angeles, the two gold medals were split between two different countries for the first time—the United States taking the team prize and Lt de Mortanges and Marcroix retaining their title—the only rider and horse ever to do so in the history of the Olympic Games.

In 1936, at the notorious Berlin Games, Germany took both the golds, Captain Stubbendorff on Nurmi winning the individual title. War then intervened and there were no more Olympic Games for twelve years until those held in London in 1948, when the gold medals were again divided between two countries. The United States regained the team honours and Captain B. M. Chevallier of France on Aiglonne taking the individual gold.

Finland, who should have staged the 1940 Olympic Games if they had been held, were hosts for the 1952 event and it was their neighbours, Sweden, who again took the double honours, the individual gold going to Captain H. von Blixen-Finecke on Jubal. Since just over eight per cent of the Finns are Swedish-speaking, this was a popular victory.

The 1956 Equestrian events were again held in Stockholm because of the quarantine regulations in Australia, where the rest of the Games were staged—and forty-four years after the Three-Day Event was first introduced into Olympic competition, the team prize went to Great Britain, who were led in masterly fashion by Colonel Frank Weldon. Once again, it was a Swedish rider, Mr P. Kastenman, on Olluster, who triumphed in the individual classification.

The Australians made their first impact on the Olympic Scene in Rome in 1960, Mr L. Morgan on Salad Days leading the team to a double triumph. Tokyo, in 1964, was the setting for another double triumph, this time by the Italians, Mr M. Checcoli, on Surbeanm pocketing the individual award.

The Olympic spotlight moved to Mexico in 1968 and for only the second time in the history of the Games, the team award went to Great Britain, so ably led by Major Allhusen on Lochinvar, winners of the individual silver medal, the gold going to M. J.-J. Guyon of France on Pitou.

Since many of the riders and horses involved in the 1968 Olympics are still active, it is interesting to study in some detail the results in Mexico. The teams finished in this order: Great Britain, 175.93 penalty points, 1; United States 245.87, 2; Australia

331.26, 3; France 505.83, 4; West Germany 518.22, 5; and Mexico 631.56, 6. The individual awards were divided as follows: M. Jean-Jacques Guyon's Pitou (France) 38.86, 1; Major D. Allhusen's Lochinvar (Great Britain) 41.61, 2; Mr M. Page's Foster (United States) 52.31, 3; Mr R. Meade's Cornishman V (Great Britain) 64.46, 4; Staff-Sergeant R. Jones's The Poacher (Great Britain) 69.86, 5.

Now world interest focuses on Munich and let it be said at once that Great Britain, on the evidence of their recent past successes, must travel to West Germany as one of the firm favourites for the team gold. No other nation can match the British team's achievements over the last five years—an Olympic title, a world title and three European titles. But the competition in Munich is sure to be intense, with the Americans and Australians always immensely strong. The Russians obviously learned a lot at Burghley last September and could well spring a surprise, while past evidence shows that the host country always has every advantage on its side—not least that its animals are saved tiring journeys.

Can Princess Anne achieve her life's ambition and make the British Olympic team? Twelve months ago she was merely a promising rider, without international experience. Then came Badminton, where she achieved fifth place in her first Open Three-Day Event—with an invitation to compete in the European Championships as her reward. Shrugging aside the interruption of her operation last July, she went on to Burghley—and as someone remarked, she could hardly do better than come first! Incidentally, it is interesting to note that Mrs Oliver, without committing herself to rash predictions, feels that the 1972 Olympics have come at just the right stage in Princess Anne's riding career.

And who is likely to win the individual gold medal in Munich? It would be foolhardy indeed to risk a forecast with so many first-class riders and horses around, especially since both riders and horses can lose their form overnight. But two points stand out in a detailed examination of the Olympic results since Stockholm in 1912—no British rider has ever taken the individual gold medal and no woman has ever won this greatest of all riding distinctions. So the question must be asked—on the sixtieth anniversary of the Three-Day Event being included in the Olympic Games, can Princess Anne become the first woman and the first British rider to win the individual gold medal? If she succeeds, spectators at the 1972 Munich Olympic Games will have a Royal Golden Girl to applaud. . . .

The lonely moment—just before the roads and tracks at Eridge.

Proud moment for Doublet at Burghley where Princess Anne was invited by the British selectors to compete in the 1971 European Championships as an "invited individual".

Watching and waiting at Eridge.

No mishap this time as Doublet splashes through. . . .

. . . clearing the tree trunk out of the water.

Princess Anne and Doublet at Badminton.

The Parade of Champions on the last day of the 1971 Horse of the Year Show at Wembley. And HRH The Princess Anne is introduced as the Champion of Europe. . . .

Auld Lang Syne at Wembley and Princess Anne joins in with other competitors, including Harvey Smith and Ann Moore, after the Parade of Champions at the 1971 Horse of the Year Show.

*Looking to future triumphs—and,
perhaps, an Olympic Gold
Medal at Munich. . . .*